SUPER ENGINEER

BUILD YOUR OWN CARS

Thanks to the creative team:

Senior Editor: Alice Peebles
Fact checking: Tom Jackson
Design: Perfect Bound Ltd

First published in Great Britain in 2018
by Hungry Tomato Ltd
PO Box 181
Edenbridge
Kent, TN8 9DP

A CIP catalogue record for this book is available
from the British Library.

ISBN 978-1-912108-60-2

Printed and bound in China

Discover more at
www.hungrytomato.com

SUPER ENGINEER

BUILD YOUR OWN CARS

BY **ROB IVES**

HUNGRY TOMATO™

SAFETY FIRST

Take care and use good sense when making these fun model vehicles – they are all quite straightforward, but you will need to cut materials, drill holes etc, for which it's handy to have an adult assistant (see below).

Every project includes a list of everything you will need to build it. Most will be stuff that you can find around the house, or is readily available and inexpensive to buy online or from a local hardware or general-purpose store.

We have also included 'How It Works' for each model, to explain in simple terms the engineering or scientific principles that make it move. And for some there is a 'Real-world Engineering' snippet that applies these principles to actual machines.

Watch out for this sign accompanying some model instructions. You may need help from an adult with completing these tasks.

DISCLAIMER

The author, publisher and bookseller cannot take responsibility for your safety. When you make and try out the projects, you do so at your own risk. Look out for the safety warning symbol (above) given throughout the book and call on adult assistance when you are cutting materials or testing out the vehicles.

CONTENTS

(Words in **bold** are explained here)

CARS

When you're out driving with your mum and dad, the car seems to go fast or slow really easily, doesn't it? Just using the accelerator or brake pedal seems to do it. But there's so much work going on under the bonnet, and it's all at the command of the driver pushing the pedals and moving the gear stick.

Now you can get into the driving seat with these eight brilliant models that operate on the very basic law that nothing will move unless it's pushed by a force! And you don't need a car engine to do that: a twisted elastic band will do the job. Combine it with two clothes pegs and you have a tiny dragster. Or add a mini motor to give extra oomph to your electric car. Even the force released by an inflated balloon produces something very like rocket power.

So get your tools and materials together, start building and see how these machines go – hey, you can even mobilize a mousetrap! Why not kick off with the football car – it shows you how car gears work...

TOP TIPS

- Before you start on any of the models, read the step-by-steps all the way through to get an idea of what you're aiming for. The pictures show what the steps tell you to do.

- Use a cutting mat or similar surface for cutting lengths off skewers etc.

- Ask for help with cutting the barrel of a pen – this can be quite tricky! One way of doing it neatly is to use a file to cut a notch all the way round, then snap off the piece.

- Use the sharp end of a pencil to make small holes in cardboard. Or ask an adult to help with this, using scissors or a craft knife.

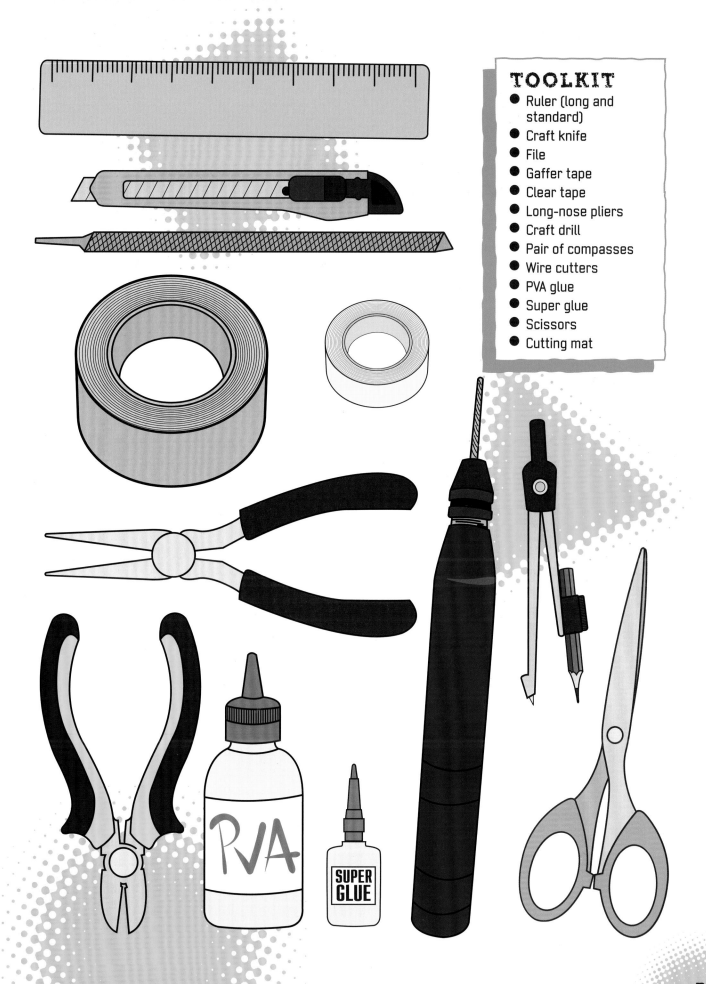

TOOLKIT
- Ruler (long and standard)
- Craft knife
- File
- Gaffer tape
- Clear tape
- Long-nose pliers
- Craft drill
- Pair of compasses
- Wire cutters
- PVA glue
- Super glue
- Scissors
- Cutting mat

PVA

SUPER GLUE

FOOTBALL CAR

A motorized football gives a whole new meaning to ball control! It's pushed along by a small companion wheel.

TOOLS:
- Scissors
- Ruler
- Super glue
- File
- Wire cutters
- Long-nose pliers

YOU WILL NEED:

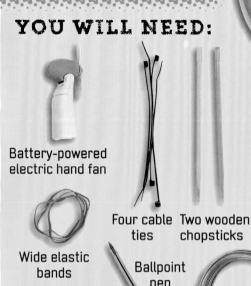

Battery-powered electric hand fan

Four cable ties

Two wooden chopsticks

Wide elastic bands

Ballpoint pen

Two roundhead screws (12 x 4mm)

Smooth 220mm plastic football

Two rubber suckers, 40mm wide (eg from a shower soap dish)

Two practice airflow golf balls

Stiff 2mm garden wire

PULL

1 Pull the fan head off the electric fan, revealing the electric motor shaft.

2 Cut an elastic band and carefully wrap it round the motor shaft, gluing it in place with super glue at the same time.. Continue adding elastic bands until the rubber wheel is roughly 40mm in diameter.

3 Fix a screw into the end of the rubber suckers so that the head is 3-4mm above the top of the sucker. Add a dot of glue to the thread as you screw it in to keep it airtight.

4 Wet the suckers and stick them to the football opposite each other. Try and get them as exactly opposite as possible.

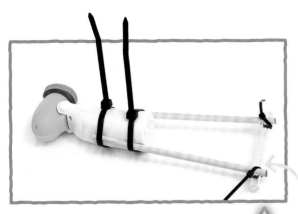

5 Discard the inner from the ballpoint pen. Cut a 50mm section from the pen body with a file (see Top Tips, page 6). Fasten the chopsticks tightly to the fan body with cable ties. Tie the pen tube to the other ends. Trim the cable tie ends with scissors.

Start up the fan motor. Place the vehicle on a smooth, flat surface (not a carpet), rest the rubber wheel on the football and watch it being driven!

ZOOOOM!

6 Use wire cutters to cut a length of wire three times the diameter of the ball. Use pliers to make a loop at one end to fit over the screw. Shape the rest of the wire as in the image below, so it slots through one golf ball, the pen tube and the other golf ball. Make another loop at the other end to fit the other screw.

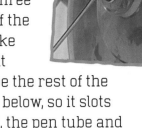

The wheel and ball should rotate in the directions shown. If not, just flip the motor over to the other side of the ball.

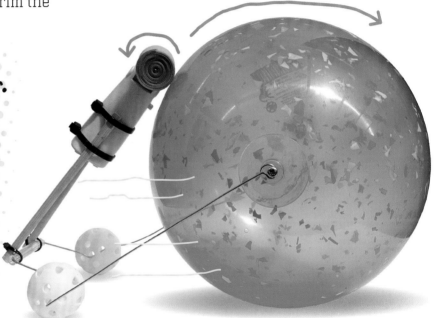

HOW IT WORKS

The ball model is powered by an electric motor. **Chemical energy** from the battery is converted into **electrical energy** and then into spinning **kinetic energy** by the electric motor. The small rubber wheel and the large football work together like a **gear** slowing down the final rotation, so the vehicle moves in a controlled way. The rubber wheel is held against the ball by **gravity**.

The gears on a car are also round and different sizes, but have toothed edges to grip each other.

ROCKET POWER

This car shoots off as the balloon loses air. It uses the same principle as rocket power: a thrust backwards creates a spurt forwards.

TOOLS:
- Ruler
- Craft knife
- Craft drill
- File
- Gaffer tape
- Scissors

YOU WILL NEED:

Balloon

Water-soluble felt-tip pen, 10–12mm wide

Four 10–12mm wooden beads

Thin poster tube, 50mm wide

Two wooden skewers

Two cable ties

Four round 75-mm plastic lids from crisp containers

1 Use a craft knife to cut a 200mm length of poster tube. Use a craft drill to drill holes slightly larger than the skewers on opposite sides, roughly 40mm from each end.

2 Cut two 90mm lengths of skewer for the **axles**. Make a small hole with a craft knife in the centre of the lids to fit the skewers tightly. Thread the skewers into the tube. Add a bead on each side as a washer.

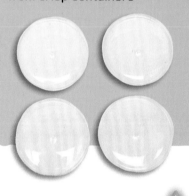

3 Fit the lid wheels onto the skewers, with the rims facing outwards.

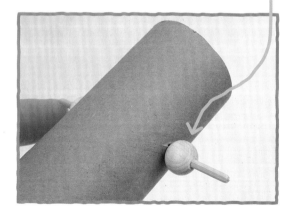

4 Remove the pen top and cut a 70mm section from the body with a file. The inner will drop out. ⚠️

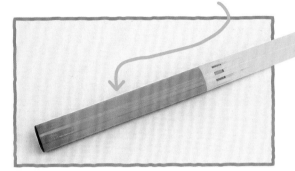

5 Fit the end of the balloon over the wider end of the pen. Tape it in place with gaffer tape.

6 Position the pen nozzle section on the poster tube end so that it extends beyond it by 10mm. Fix it in place with two cable ties. Trim the ends of the ties with scissors.

7 Inflate the balloon by blowing into the pen nozzle. Pinch the balloon end above the nozzle, place the rocket car on a smooth surface and...

...release!

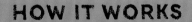

WHOOSH!

HOW IT WORKS

When the balloon is released, the elastic of the balloon pushes air out of the nozzle, and the car shoots forward, just like a rocket! It's an example of **Newton's Third Law of Motion**: every action has an equal and opposite reaction. So a rocket shoots out burning gases (the action) with a force to give it lift-off (the reaction).

ELECTRIC CAN CAR

The Model T Ford got the nickname Tin Lizzie in 1922, when it beat lots of fancier cars in a race – though it looked like a tin can! This tin can car can really go, too!

TOOLS:
- Long ruler
- Pair of compasses
- Kitchen scissors
- Clear tape
- Craft drill
- File
- Wire cutters
- Long-nose pliers
- PVA glue

YOU WILL NEED:

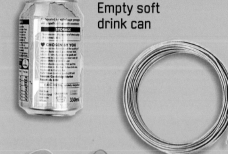
Empty soft drink can

Offcuts of corrugated cardboard

Stiff 2mm garden wire

Electric motor

Battery box with switch

Assorted elastic bands

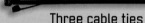
Three cable ties

Thin felt-tip pen, roughly 7mm in diameter

Two wooden skewers

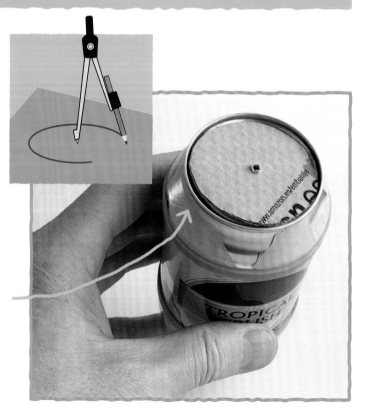

1 Rinse out and thoroughly dry the drink can. Find two wide elastic bands that fit tightly round the can. These will act as tyres.

2 Measure the diameter of the open end of the can. With a pair of compasses and scissors, make a circle of corrugated card to fit just inside the rim of the tin. Make a hole in the centre with a skewer. Tape the card in place.

3 Make a hole in the centre of the other end of the can with a craft drill. Thread a wooden skewer from the bottom and up through the card circle.

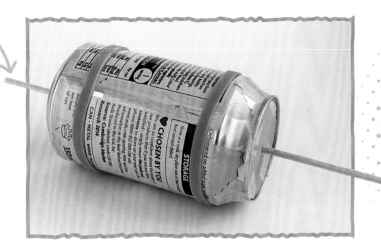

4 Connect the battery box to the motor and give it a test run. The shaft on the motor will be the drive shaft. Keep the battery and motor connected.

5 Cut an 80mm length of tube from the pen with a file. Use a cable tie to wrap together the motor, battery and tube. Trim the tie with scissors.

6 Fit a loose-fitting, thin elastic band round the tin between the other two elastic bands. This will be your drive belt.

7 Use wire cutters to cut a length of garden wire about 600mm long. Use pliers to form a loop at each end and shape it as shown to make a mounting carriage for the motor. Slot the loops over the skewer.

The mounting carriage is slightly off-centre, so the drive shaft from the motor is close to the centre.

Slip the thin elastic band over the motor drive shaft.

8 Use two cable ties to secure the motor and battery on the mounting carriage. Trim the ends of the ties.

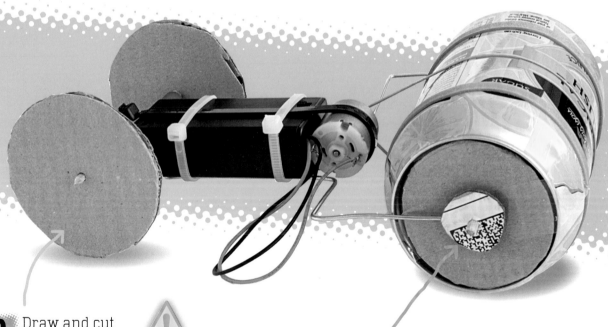

9 Draw and cut out four circles, roughly 50mm in diameter, from corrugated card. Glue them in pairs with PVA glue to make the wheels. Make holes in the centres with a skewer. Slot the skewer through the pen tube and fit on the wheels.

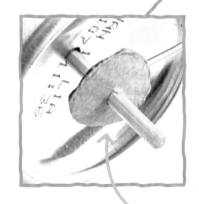

10 Make two cardboard washers, 20mm in diameter. Fit them over the can skewer to keep the wire in place. Trim all the skewer ends with wire cutters.

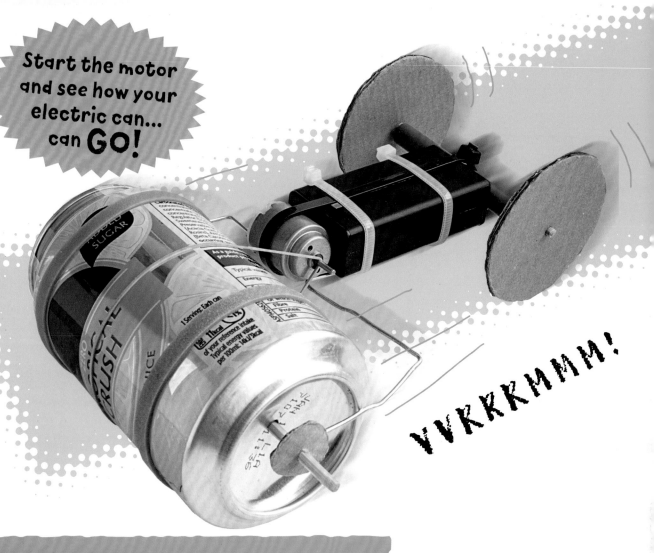

Start the motor and see how your electric can... can GO!

VVRRRMMM!

HOW IT WORKS

The battery powers the motor to spin its shaft, turning the thin elastic band to move the can. The thick elastic bands around the can work like tyres. Rubber has a high co-efficient of **friction** meaning it grips firmly only the surface it is resting on. The small drive shaft of the motor, the body of the can and the thin elastic band work as the drive system.

REAL-WORLD ENGINEERING

When a car engine is turned on, fuel burns and becomes a hot gas, which expands. The energy from the expanded gas pushes down pistons in the engine and creates kinetic energy – energy from movement. Kinetic energy is transferred through the drive system to the wheels to make them rotate.

DYNAMIC DRAGSTER

The power from a stretched elastic band mimics the dramatic acceleration of dragsters: cars that race over very short distances.

TOOLS:
- Ruler
- Wire cutters
- Long-nose pliers
- Scissors

YOU WILL NEED:

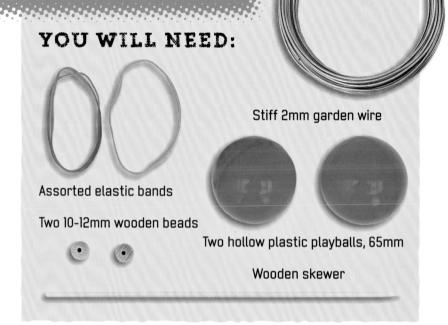

Assorted elastic bands

Two 10-12mm wooden beads

Stiff 2mm garden wire

Two hollow plastic playballs, 65mm

Wooden skewer

1 Pierce holes in opposite sides of the ball pool balls with the point of the skewer. Make sure they will fit tightly on the skewer.

POKE

2 Use wire cutters to cut a 300mm length of wire. Thread on the wooden beads, then shape it with pliers into a square-ended U to hold the beads. Make small loops at the ends. Thread the skewer through the balls and the wire loops.

3 For the tyres, choose two wide elastic bands that fit neatly round the centre of the balls.

4 Cut a 50mm length of wire and use the pliers to bend it into an S shape.

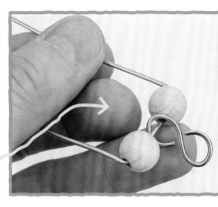

5 Fit the S wire between the two beads.

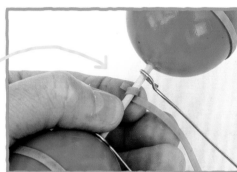

6 Select a long, wide elastic band and cut it open. Tie one end securely to the free end of the S wire.

7 Wrap the other end tightly round the skewer. Roll the wheels to stretch the band so that it's under tension.

Release the band to launch your dragster!

POW!

HOW IT WORKS

Dragsters **accelerate** as fast as possible, usually for just 402 m (1,320 ft) to reach the finish line. Energy in this model is stored in the stretched elastic band. When the dragster is released, a **restoring force** returns the band to its unstretched length. This force spins the wheels so the model whizzes away.

MOVING MOUSETRAP

Relative to its size, the spring in a mousetrap is energy-packed. It has to be, to catch mice! Here you harness that snappy speed by turning it into a car!

TOOLS:
- Craft drill
- Ruler
- Kitchen scissors
- Clear tape
- PVA glue
- Pair of compasses
- Long-nose pliers

YOU WILL NEED:

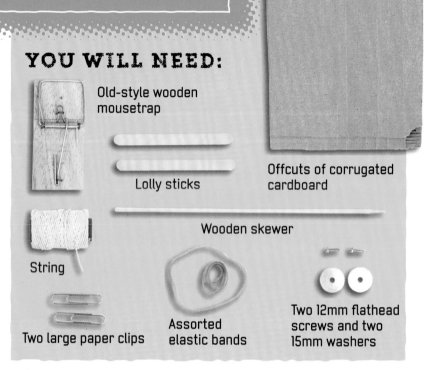

Old-style wooden mousetrap

Lolly sticks

Offcuts of corrugated cardboard

Wooden skewer

String

Two large paper clips

Assorted elastic bands

Two 12mm flathead screws and two 15mm washers

1 Use a craft drill to make a hole in the end of the lolly sticks slightly wider than the skewer.

Cut a 70mm length of cardboard slightly narrower than the base of the mousetrap. Cut a 70mm length of skewer for the axle. Wrap the cardboard tightly round it and tape it in place.

Fit the axle and lolly sticks together. Glue the sticks to the sides of the mousetrap with PVA glue. Use elastic bands to hold it all in place as it dries.

Axle

2 Cut out six 70mm cardboard circles. Glue them in threes back to back to make two wheels. Choose elastic bands wide enough to wrap around the wheels as tyres.

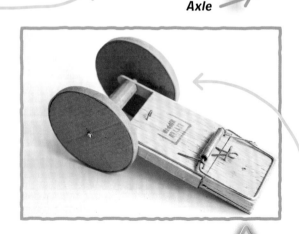

3 Using the tip of the scissors, make holes in the centre of the wheels to fit snugly over the axle ends. Glue the wheels to the axle.

4 Cut out and glue two 40mm circles of cardboard for the front wheel. Fit it with an axle made from a 40mm length of skewer. Use pliers to straighten out the paper clips and make a loop at one end of each. Slot the loops over the axle.

5 Drill a small pilot hole centrally in the mousetrap base and another 30mm away. Screw in the two washers to trap the paper clip wires and hold the front wheel in place.

6 Tie a 200mm length of string to the swing arm of the mousetrap.

7 Wrap the string round the axle, pulling it so that the swing arm pulls back. Fit the trigger in the normal way for a mousetrap. Take care! It could bite!

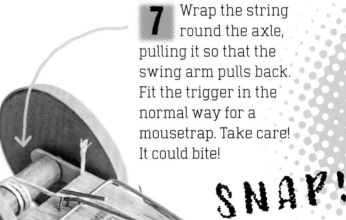

Trigger

SNAP!

Tap the trigger with a pencil or chopstick – and launch!

HOW IT WORKS

All vehicles work by converting some sort of stored energy into kinetic energy (energy from movement). In the mousetrap, the steel spring works as the energy store. When the mousetrap is triggered, the string round the axle is pulled, spinning the wheels to propel the car forwards.

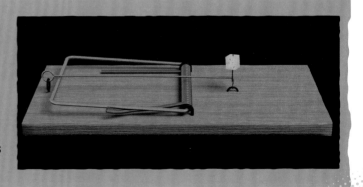

CLOTHES PEG MICRO CAR

One clothes peg is the car, the other is the 'trigger' that catapults it into movement. Try it out on a smooth surface – make more than one and have a race!

TOOLS:
- Long-nose pliers
- Wire cutters
- Craft knife
- PVA glue

YOU WILL NEED:

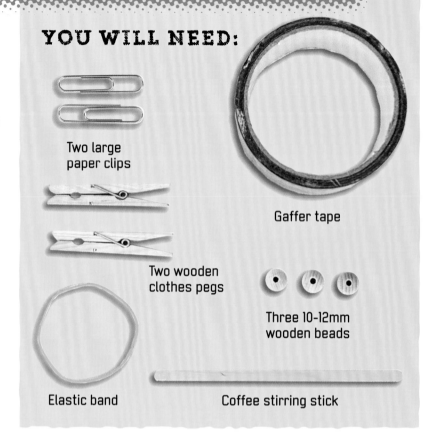

Two large paper clips

Gaffer tape

Two wooden clothes pegs

Three 10-12mm wooden beads

Elastic band

Coffee stirring stick

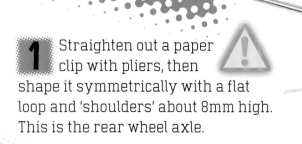

PRESS

1 Straighten out a paper clip with pliers, then shape it symmetrically with a flat loop and 'shoulders' about 8mm high. This is the rear wheel axle.

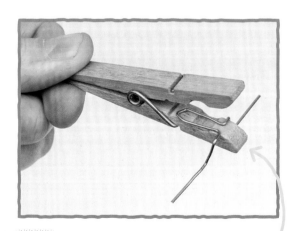

2 Position the axle in the peg as shown and close the peg to hold it in place.

3 Straighten out the second paper clip and thread one of the wooden beads into the centre. Fold the paper clip to make a flat-bottomed U shape holding the bead. This is the front axle.

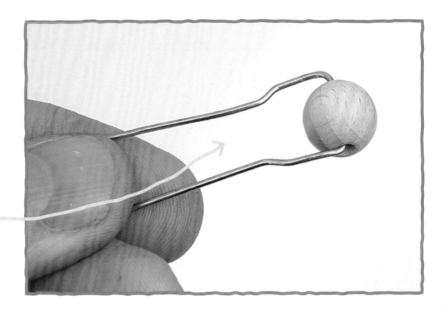

4 Use wire cutters to trim the paper clip wire to fit along the edges of the other end of the clothes peg. Tape it in place with gaffer tape. (The rear axle is not shown here.)

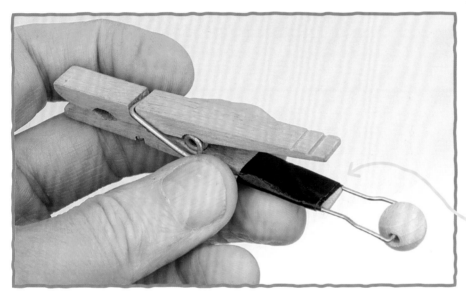

5 With the rear axle in position, slot the wooden beads on either side. Bend up the ends to hold them in place and snip off the excess wire with wire cutters.

6 Cut a length of coffee stirring stick slightly longer than the peg. Cut a notch in one end with a craft knife and use PVA glue to fix it to the base of the peg as shown.

7 Wrap an elastic band around the second clothes peg, tying the end if necessary to make it taut. This acts as the trigger.

8 Push the end of the coffee stick into the elastic band and hold it with the peg. Press the peg open to launch your peg car!

HOW IT WORKS

The power that drives this car is separate from the car itself. A quick elastic kick from the peg trigger shoots the vehicle on its way. The wire axles and bead wheels have very low friction so after the initial kick, the car runs for a surprising distance.

KER-POW!

REAL-WORLD ENGINEERING

An elastic material is one that can be deformed a lot but always springs back to its original shape. This is why a hand-held catapult uses an elastic band. The elastic is stretched backwards to make it as taut as possible. This stretching stores energy in the band. When the band is released, it pings back into shape, and the energy is transferred to the **projectile** as kinetic energy, so it flies off.

PROPELLER POWER

If propellers give aircraft lift-off and keep them in the air, why not harness that power to move a car? In fact, an inventor called Clifford Robbins did just that in 1955, using a large propeller attached to the back of a small car to get it to speeds of 70 mph (112 km/h) – though it also had a small engine!

TOOLS:
- Long-nose pliers
- Long ruler
- Wire cutters
- Scissors
- Craft knife

YOU WILL NEED:

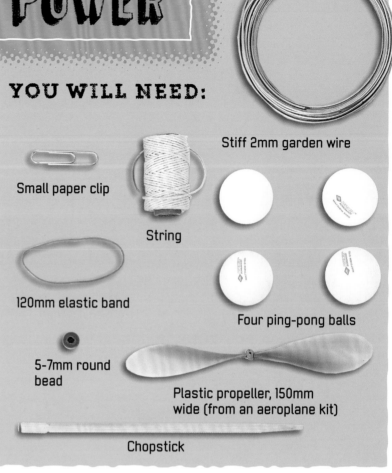

Small paper clip

String

Stiff 2mm garden wire

120mm elastic band

Four ping-pong balls

5-7mm round bead

Plastic propeller, 150mm wide (from an aeroplane kit)

Chopstick

1 Use the pliers to straighten out the paper clip and bend a loop in the end.

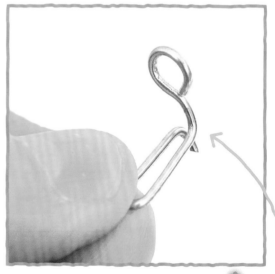

2 Cut a 70mm length of garden wire and make a support in the shape shown.

3 Thread the paper clip wire through the support loop, then the bead and finally the propeller.

4 Bend the end of the paper clip wire to make a right angle to hold it in place. Trim the end with wire cutters.

5 To make the front legs, cut a 350mm length of garden wire, and use the pliers to bend it symmetrically into the shape shown. The doubled bit is about 20mm long, and roughly at right angles to the legs.

6 Position the legs and propeller support on the end of the chopstick. Hold them in place by wrapping string around and secure the end.

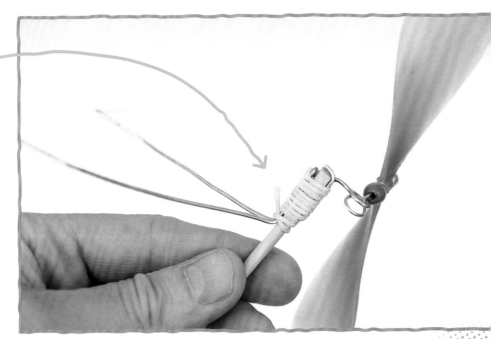

7 Cut another 350mm piece of wire and shape the back legs as shown. The hook section is about 50mm long overall, and will stop the legs being pulled forward.

⚠️

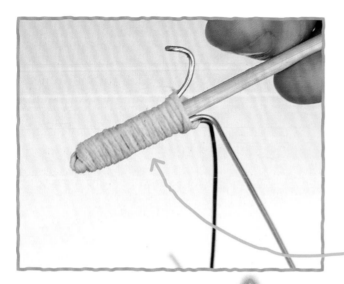

8 Bind the looped end of the legs to the other end of the chopstick with string, leaving the hook free.

9 Use a craft knife to make holes in the four ping-pong balls that will take the wire legs. Thread the balls onto the wire legs. Bend the legs up at the end to trap the balls in position, then cut off any excess wire.

⚠️

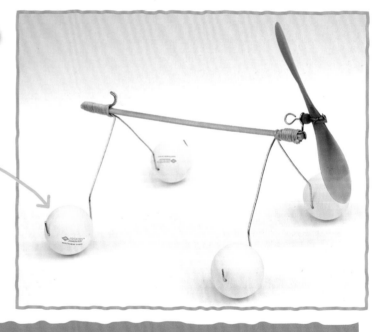

Spin direction

Angled blades push air back

Car is pushed forwards

HOW IT WORKS

Many vehicles are driven via their wheels. Not so with the propeller car. Energy to drive the propeller car is stored in the stretch of the twisted elastic band. As the propeller spins, air is forced backwards, pushing the car forwards. The long legs stop the propeller touching the ground.

10 Twist the elastic band and fit it between the hook at the back of the car and the loop behind the propeller. Wind up the propeller and...

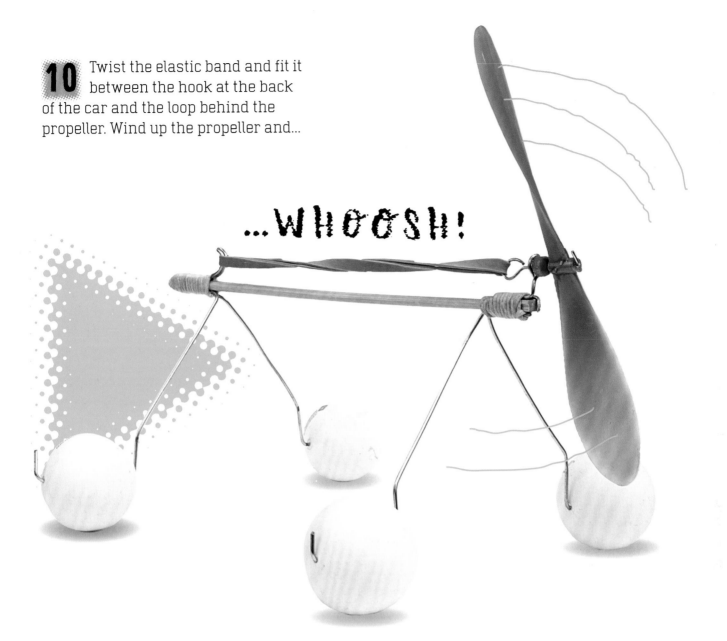

...WHOOSH!

REAL-WORLD ENGINEERING

A spinning aeroplane propeller pushes back masses of air, and this continuous pushing gets the plane moving. A propeller's blades are both twisted and angled, and the more steeply they're angled, the more air they push back and the more the plane moves forward. This also shows Newton's Third Law of Motion in action: a push backwards produces a movement forwards.

TRIKE-ERRIFIC!

This brilliant tricycle has front-wheel drive like lots of cars that have to go over rough terrain. The golf ball wheels work best on a nice smooth surface, though!

TOOLS:
- Scissors
- Craft knife
- File
- Ruler
- Pair of compasses
- PVA glue

YOU WILL NEED:

Two wide elastic bands, 50mm and 70mm

Airflow practice golf balls

Corrugated cardboard offcut

Two pencils

Two felt-tip pens

Wooden skewer

Four cable ties

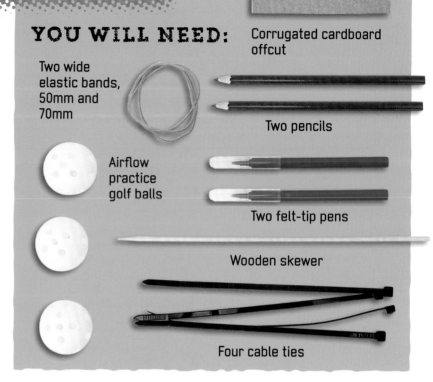

1 Cut the 70mm elastic band and thread it through two symmetrical holes on either side of a ball. Tie the ends together.

2 Use a craft knife to cut a notch near each end of the pencils on one side.

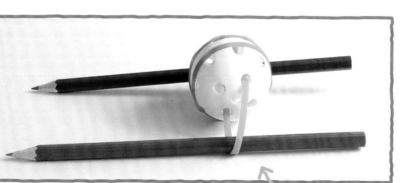

3 Wrap the 50mm elastic band twice round the ball for the tyre. Thread the pencils through the central elastic band.

4 Remove the tops and inners from the pens. ⚠ Cut the ends off with a file, to a length of about 90mm. Use cable ties to fasten the tubes in the pencil notches.

6 Draw and cut ⚠ out two card circles, 20mm in diameter, to act as washers. Pierce holes in the centres with the point of the skewer, and glue them in place. Cut off any excess skewer.

5 Thread a wooden skewer through the rear tube and slot the two remaining balls in place. Trim the cable ties with scissors.

Z-Z-ZIPP!

Wind up the front wheel by turning it several times – and release!

HOW IT WORKS

Just like the propeller car, the trike stores its energy in twisted elastic. This time though, the untwisting drives the front wheel directly, pushing the car forwards. The rubber band tyre ensures a good grip as the trike moves, just like a car tyre on the road surface.

GLOSSARY

ACCELERATION (VERB: ACCELERATE)

The rate at which an object changes speed. Positive acceleration is an increase in speed, negative acceleration a decrease in speed.

AXLE

A central rod that a vehicle's wheels fit on to and keeps them an equal distance apart. It rotates to make the wheels rotate so the vehicle can move.

CHEMICAL ENERGY

The energy stored in chemical compounds, which is released by a chemical reaction. For example, when wood burns (creating a chemical reaction) the chemical energy turns into heat and light energy. Batteries, natural gas and petroleum all have masses of stored chemical energy.

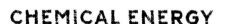

ELECTRICAL ENERGY

The energy that moves charged particles through a wire. This flow of energy is called a current and can be converted to perform all sorts of work such as making light, heat or sound. An electric motor converts electrical energy into kinetic energy, the energy of motion.

ENERGY

The ability to apply force to move an object or do work.

FRICTION

A force that works against an object sliding along a surface. For example, a ball rolling along a road will eventually stop because of friction from the road's surface.

GEARS

The circular, interlocking wheels in an engine that help to control the vehicle's speed. They work with the throttle, which controls the speed at which the engine rotates. The range of speed in first gear might go up to 15mph, in second up to 25mph, in third up to 40mph, and so on. A lower gear therefore gives more power and a higher gear more speed.

GRAVITY

The force that pulls objects towards each other. The larger the object, the stronger is its force of gravity. This is why things stay in place on the Earth's surface unless they are shot off, with a huge amount of force, into space.

KINETIC ENERGY

The energy that all moving objects have. The amount of energy depends on an object's mass and speed.

NEWTON'S THIRD LAW OF MOTION

The physical law that states 'every action has an equal and opposite reaction' – that is, a push backwards creates an equal push forwards, or vice versa. The great scientist Isaac Newton published this law in 1687, along with his first two laws about how forces relate to motion.

PROJECTILE

Any object fired or thrown into the air by a force.

RESTORING FORCE

The force that returns a system or material to its original shape or position, after it has been pulled or misshapen. For example, a spring that has been elongated will return to its natural shape and length by its own restoring force.

INDEX

THE AUTHOR

Rob Ives is a former maths and science teacher, now a designer and paper engineer living in Cumbria, UK. He creates science- and project-based children's books, including *Paper Models that Rock!* and *Paper Automata*. He specializes in character-based paper animations and all kinds of fun and fascinating science projects, and often visits schools to talk about design technology and demonstrate his models. Rob's other series for Hungry Tomato include *Tabletop Battles* and *Amazing Science Experiments*.

Picture Credits

(abbreviations: t = top; b = bottom; c = centre; l = left; r = right)

Shutterstock.com: Alex Mit 15br, Anatoly Vartanov 29br, bunnyphoto 23br, Dmitry Minein 6tr, Igor Maltsev 19br, John A Davis 11br & 31tr, nikkytok 9br & 31tl, Phillip Rubino 17bl, Radoslaw Maciejewski 27bl